ISBN 978-0-484-37826-0
PIBN 10253229

This book is a reproduction of an important historical work. Forgotten Books uses
state-of-the-art technology to digitally reconstruct the work, preserving the original format
whilst repairing imperfections present in the aged copy. In rare cases, an imperfection in
the original, such as a blemish or missing page, may be replicated in our edition. We do,
however, repair the vast majority of imperfections successfully; any imperfections that
remain are intentionally left to preserve the state of such historical works.

Persiatic...
Preparations

PREPARED BY

The Pickhardt Renfrew Co.
Limited

STOUFFVILLE, ONT.

THE SENTINEL PRINT
STOUFFVILLE

ISSUED BY
PICKHARDT RENFREW CO., Limited

▼

Stouffville, Ont., Can., May, 1899

We believe, in presenting this pamphlet to the farmer, stock breeder, housewife, and the public, that our interest is also your interest. We have endeavored to say a little on each subject— the cow, the horse, the pig and the sheep, your carpets and clothes, your sick room where disease germs loiter, and also your flowering plants, shrubs and fruit trees. We come to you to destroy that which is damaging and destroying what you are undoubtedly endeavoring to protect. Space prevents us from entering into details, so we deal direct with facts only. We know it to be to your interest to study the contents of this pamphlet, and to retain it until our next issue. We shall, from time to time, give you interesting reading matter. We intend to have you write to us on any subject that comes under the heading of our products. We repeat we want you interested in our affairs, and to know that what is beneficial to you is likewise the same to us. We want you to look forward to our next issue with interest. We shall endeavor to keep you in touch with ourselves. Correspondence always solicited.

The Persiatic Specialties represent a line of goods of well-established merit and standard purity. They are prepared under the supervision of chemists and experts at our own extensive laboratories in Stouffville, and fill their various purposes in a manner unapproached by any other articles in the market to-day. They have only to be shown to create a demand for themselves—they fill urgent needs in the household and on the farm in the way of getting rid of insect life, fungi, disease germs, and curing skin diseases in cattle, horses, sheep, pigs, dogs and poultry.

The Persiatic Specialties are being well and liberally advertised, and the sales are proving the confidence the public have in the quickness and thoroughness with which they do their work.

THE PICKHARDT RENFREW CO., Limited

STOUFFVILLE, ONT., CAN.

Persiatic Horse Wash

....JUST A MOMENT....

We know your time is valuable. So is everybody's. We find it so. We spent a few valuable moments preparing this pamphlet, for your benefit as well as our own. If you own a horse, which most likely you do, it is then your duty and pleasure to look after his appearance and comfort. We are going to say just as little as possible, so as not to tire you with useless reading matter. We have spent a large amount of money on Persiatic Horse Wash to bring it to that high standard it has obtained. We say it with no little pride, that Persiatic Horse Wash does do all we claim for it, and that it excels anything and everything of its kind on the market to-day. It is the very best curative for all skin diseases, it is the very best tonic, it is the very best thing to clean the skin of nits and vermin and brighten the pelt as no other remedy has done or can do. The care, the work, the knowledge, the machinery, expert chemists and veterinarians employed to perfect Persiatic Horse Wash, leaves no room for doubt to our claim.

An antiseptic and healing preparation of highly concentrated curative qualities for use on horses in all skin diseases and attacks of vermin. Cures Scratches, Bruises, Mange, Ringworm, Grease, Eczema, Papules, Uticarea, Pityriases, etc. Has no drastic or irritating effects and cures the worst cases. Invaluable for use in cases of all insect pests.

Mr. Robert Graham, one of Canada's great horse fanciers, and judge at the Madison Square Horse Show, New York, says :

" Some weeks ago we found one of our Draft Brood Mares was very itchy and scurvy in the legs. From the good reports we had heard of your Persiatic Horse Wash, we concluded to try it. We have found it an excellent preparation, having made three applications on mare's legs, and can say it has perfectly healed the leg and eradicated all itchy symptoms. We can recommend it to all horsemen for skin diseases on horses, and believe if used according to direcuions it will cure most obstinate cases."

N. B —Mr. Robert Graham, of Messrs. Graham Bros., was appointed judge at the last Great Horse Show held at Madison Square Garden, New York City. This exceptional honor conferred on a Canadian speaks volumes. The high standing of Messrs. Graham Bros., of Claremont, Ont., in Canada, the United States and Great Britain will leave no question of doubt about their testimonial and should recommend Persiatic Horse Wash to all horse owners, breeders, dealers and farmers. Persiatic Horse Wash is a remedy that should always be kept on hand, and the moment any symptoms of skin diseases appear, it should immediately be applied. Persiatic Horse Wash is endorsed by the highest horse fancier authorities as the only Common-Sense Wash for all skin diseases on Horses and Cattle.

Price, $1 00 per 34 oz. can.
Sample cans, 25 and 50 cents.

STOUFFVILLE, ONT., Feb. 20th, 1899.
THE PICKHARDT RENFREW CO., Stouffville, Ont.

Gentlemen,—Having used all sorts of remedies for scratches on horses, and with no success whatever, I concluded that which could not "be cured must be endured." I recently heard of your Persiatic Horse Wash and concluded to try it. After using it a few days according to directions, horses so affected were completely cured. I have since heard the very best reports on Persiatic Horse Wash and am also pleased to add my praises.

(Signed) ELIJAH PENNOCK,
Stouffville Livery Stables

Persiatic Sheep Dip and Animal Wash

Awarded Bronze Medals and Diplomas at Toronto, London, Ottawa, Sherbrooke and other leading fairs of Canada, 1898.

A powerful non-irritant and healing preparation for the cure of all Skin Diseases affecting Sheep and Cattle, and for destroying Vermin. It is manufactured under the supervision of skilled Chemists, and warranted free from harmful ingredients. Cures sores, bruises, boils, gangrene, wounds, shear cuts, ringworm, scab, etc., and makes the skin whole and sound. Leaves the animal refreshed and in good spirits after use and improves the coat. Also Persiatic Lamb Dip for Lambs. Specially prepared to destroy lice, ticks and nits, and also to be applied after castrating.

Mr. G. A. Brodie, a prominent Stock Raiser of Bethesda, Ont., says :—

BETHESDA, ONT., October 20th, 1898.

THE PICKHARDT RENFREW CO., Stouffville, Ont.

Gentlemen,—After having used a number of cans of your Persiatic Sheep and Animal Dip, I am free to say that it is the best Dip I have ever used. It goes further and does better work than any other. It is certainly the Dip I shall use in future. I would also say that recently I castrated a number of lambs the worst time of the year, and I must say that your Dip healed wounds rapidly, and kept maggots out. I firmly believe that yours is the very best all-round Dip on the market to-day, and recommend same accordingly.

(Signed) G. A. BRODIE.

Every farmer should have it on hand for his live stock. Strong dips used on lambs causes the ewes to refuse sucking. After castrating only use Persiatic Lamb Wash on calves, lambs, colts, and other young animals.

BALSAM, ONT., February 7th, 1899.

THE PICKHARDT RENFREW CO., Stouffville, Ont.

Gentlemen,—I am in receipt of your letter inquiring my opinion of your Persiatic Dip. We have used it with entire satisfaction and found it very effectual, equal to any dip we have ever used, if not superior, and it is only to be used to be appreciated. Yours truly,

JAMES I. DAVIDSON & SON.

Per M.M.

STOUFFVILLE, ONT., January 27th, 1899.

THE PICKHARDT RENFREW CO., LTD., Stouffville, Ont.

Gentlemen,—The question has often been put to me in my practice as Veterinary Surgeon, whether I could recommend Persiatic Sheep and Animal Wash as against other preparations of a similar nature. For the purpose of finally settling this question satisfactorily, I can say, in all my experience I have had better all-round results from Persiatic Sheep and Animal Wash than with any other preparation of a similar nature. This you are free to publish. Yours truly,

(Signed) P. G. BUTTON, V.S.

STOUFFVILLE, ONT., March 28th, 1899.

MESSRS. PICKHARDT RENFREW CO., Stouffville, Ont.

Gentlemen,—In reply to your inquiry re your Persiatic Sheep and Animal Wash, we are pleased to state it has given us every satisfaction. We have recommended it to our neighbors. We consider it a necessary article to keep on the farm and shall always have some on hand. For destroying insects and healing sore skins it has no equal. Yours truly,

(Signed) STOKES BROS., Mount Albert, Ont.

STOCK BREEDERS.

Sheep Scab,
and . . . .
How to Treat It

This is a disease not generally well known to the average Farmer, and its first symptoms are usually attributed to lice or vermin, manifested by an uneasiness by the Sheep so infected. About the first thing noticed is the pawing with hind foot between the fore legs. Another symptom is the pulling of wool, also the constant desire to rub up against rail fences or buildings. So annoying does the disease become that the Sheep soon lose flesh and eventually their appetite. When this stage is reached the matter becomes alarming, and generally ends fatally, as vitality is about gone. It is a well-known fact that the disease is highly

contagious, and the moment it is noticed, Sheep so infected should be isolated. We recommend the simple treatment of immediately shearing the Sheep closely, putting them in warm quarters with good ventilation (if Scab appears in winter), feeding them on substantial food. After Sheep have been sheared the scab or sores should be carefully looked for and broken up, so that each sore is open. Prepare Persiatic Sheep Dip previous to breaking sores, so as to have it ready for dipping the moment all the sores on Sheep are broken, by taking one part Persiatic Sheep

9

Dip and twenty parts tepid water. Have a vat large enough to stand sheep in so as to cover whole body, holding nose above bath and leaving Sheep stand in bath from three to five minutes. This operation should be repeated every three or four days· Sheep should be kept housed until all symptoms of disease have disappeared. When Sheep have Scab they should be taken in hand immediately. If part of flock have not got the Scab, but have been in contact with Scabby Sheep, they should all be dipped two or three times in the same solution, in a different vat and place, so that they will not come into further contact with the Scabby part of the flock until all are thoroughly well. It is wise to shear all Sheep in the flock, even if only one or two are Scabby, and all should be dipped in a solution of Persiatic Sheep Dip in proportions as above mentioned. If one Sheep in the flock has Scab it follows that the balance of the flock will sooner or later develop it. Scab is considered the most contagious and fatal disease among Sheep and should be looked for. This article was prepared under instructions of one of Canada's foremost Fancy Sheep Breeders. For Lice, Nits and Vermin on Sheep and all animals, Persiatic Sheep Dip, used according to directions, will do its work perfectly.

Persiatic Plant Spray

**Awarded Bronze Medal and Diplomas
At Toronto, Ottawa, London and Sherbrooke.**

It has been a matter of much concern of recent years to get a plant spray that would effectively destroy all kinds of insects that infest trees, shrubs, flowering plants and vegetables and which would not destroy the plant or tree on which used, and also not be a menace to human or animal life. We place before the public our Persiatic Plant Spray, which from practical trials made by experienced men has proven a perfect spray on all kinds of vegetation, for the destruction of insect life, and in no wise be destructive to the plant or tree on which used. Expense is a matter also to be taken into consideration. If Persiatic Plant Spray is used judiciously, it is as inexpensive as any spray that has been before the public. A spraying apparatus that will throw a mist is most advantageous and in the long run pays for itself. As a rule cheap spraying devices have been used, proving an actual loss of four-fifths of liquid spray being used. Frequent spraying with a non-poisonous liquid to the plants has proven most effective. Persiatic Plant Spray is a food to vegetation in so far that it is stimulating to the leaves. We are not prepared to recommend any particular spraying device, but a sprayer that will throw a fine mist is under all circumstances the best. One gallon of water should cover a good-sized apple tree if properly applied. We have seen many instances where five gallons of spray were used on one tree and most disastrous effect to the tree. All goods put up by us bear our registered trade marks and designs, a guarantee of strength and quality.

The most effective and highly concentrated spray in the market. Has successfully coped with the dreaded San Jose Scale, and readily destroys all orchard and garden pests such as grubs, worms, brown-rot, curled leaf, caterpillars, and all forms of animal life or fungi. Contains no mineral poisons such as Arsenic or Paris Green, and is endorsed by leading gardeners and nurserymen all over Canada. **Price 65 Cents Per Can**.

Mr. Daniel B. Hoover, Almira, Ont., says:

" I have used your Persiatic Plant Spray and find it works to perfection. In three applications it killed every insect on plants infested to the extent that I counted 24 insects on a single leaf. I heartily recommend your preparation, it is sure death to insects."

Persiatic Plant Food
REGISTERED

If you want beautiful flowers, strong and healthy plants, insure success of growth by apply Persiatic Plant Food when plants are young.

Our trade marks should be on all wrappers and packages, which is a guarantee of standard goods.

Persiatic Plant Food is made specially for rose bushes, shrubs, grape vines, and all tender plants requiring care, and artificial goods, to strengthen them and to give strength and vitality to the roots, which is a lasting and practically a permanent benefit to the plant.

Persiatic Plant Food is prepared from the very best imported tobaccos, from which by our own special process (known only to ourselves) all poisonous substances have been removed, leaving a food for plants that will improve their growth and prevent them from becoming diseased at the roots. This preparation is also a safe preventive which will positively defend all kinds of plants from the attacks of cut worms and other insects that injure or destroy their roots.

Persiatic Henhouse Spray
AND POULTRY POWDER.

Kill vermin in all feathered stock, and keep their quarters clear of insect pests. Lice and vermin are the most tenacious and annoying enemies to deal with in fowls. Persiatic Poultry Powder quickly destroys all vermin in fowls—with no drastic effects; and Persiatic Poultry Spray, used on the walls and roosts eradicates all traces of insects, acting also as a disinfectant, destroying disease germs and keeping the atmosphere clear of disease germs, gases and vapors.

R. P. COULSON, Stouffville, says :

"Since using your Henhouse Spray in my henhouse, everything in the shape of vermin has disappeared. I also use it as a disinfectant and deodorizer, and firmly believe it has no equal."

Persiatic Dog Wash

Remember
Healing
Refreshing
Antiseptic
Cleansing

The many skin troubles and sores of all natures to which a dog is subject have been taken into consideration in the preparation and manufacture of our Persiatic Dog Wash. It is healing, it is antiseptic, it is cleansing, it is refreshing to the animal on which it is used. Expert chemists are employed in our Laboratories in the preparation of this Wash, and we do not hesitate to say that it is the best and most effective skin wash for all animals on the market to-day.

All goods put up by us bear our registered trade marks and designs—a guarantee of purity and strength.

Awards—Bronze Medal : Toronto ; Diplomas : London and Ottawa. **Price, 25 cents**.

Office of HART & RIDDELL, Wholesale Stationers,
TORONTO, ONT., Feb. 28th, 1899.
THE PICKHARDT RENFREW CO., LIMITED, Stouffville, Ont.

Dear Sirs,—I have much pleasure in telling you that I have tried your "Persiatic Dog Wash" on my collie dog, and was quite surprised to find how well it acted in not only cleansing thoroughly but having a beneficial effect on the dog's spirits. I certainly think you have a good thing in your Dog Wash and can highly recommend it.

Yours truly,

(Signed) S. R. HART.

PERSIATIC = = = POULTRY POWDER,

If used as per directions, will quickly free poultry and poultry houses from all kinds of vermin cheaply and thoroughly. It is a safe and sure remedy for lice of all kinds on anything and anywhere. It is harmless to human and animal life. For setting hens it is especially recommended. It will not injure chickens, eggs or chicks, but it will soon rid the nest and hens of vermin. If used liberally during the hatching season, it will ensure the lives of many little chicks that would otherwise succumb to vermin. When poultry-keeping does not pay, lice is often the cause ; they worry their victims and subtract vitality that should go into flesh and eggs. They weaken the fowls, and thus make them a very easy prey to disease. The use of this powder not only kills the lice, but purifies the premises and wards off distempers and all kinds of disease.

Recommended by Poultry Editors, Judges and Breeders all over the land. **Price, 25 cents.**

Persiatic Fly & Insect Powder

Awards—Bronze Medal and Diplomas, Toronto, Ottawa and London.

This Powder is prepared specially for use in houses and other buildings for the purpose of ridding the premises of that well-known pest "the house fly." Persiatic Fly Powder is also most effective for roaches, ants and other insects that infest houses and outbuildings where live stock and fowl are housed.

All goods put up by us bear our registered trade marks and designs, a guarantee of purity and strength.

We do not hesitate to say that our Persiatic Fly and Insect Powder is the best and most effective Powder manufactured. **Price—25 cts. per box.**

PERSIATIC
.. Carpet and Cloth Powder ..

The Only True Powder that will Positively Keep Moths out of Furs, Carpets and Clothing.

This Powder is prepared and put up by our own special and expert chemists in our own laboratories. The formulæ used are a combination of long years of experience, resulting in a product that has the merits as claimed in our printed statements on the package. The purifying and germ-destroying properties of this powder, after using under carpets or in clothing, will last twelve months.

If this powder is properly and judiciously used, you can consider yourself exempt from disease and insects in your house, besides having a pure atmosphere to breathe. We claim that this Powder is made on principles to insure its constant use whenever occasion may require, giving the desired results as set forth in our claims.

A special feature is the pleasant and fresh odors that permeate rooms where used. Specially adapted to sick rooms.

This Powder is made from the very finest importations of Havana, Manila and Sumatra plants, making a combination which insures a speedy relief from all insects that infest carpets or cloth-ing, and at the same time is a destroyer of germs of all diseases that find lodgment in carpets or clothing. It is a known fact that the germs of disease find lodgment in clothing, and especially so in carpets. This is a point that we wish to impress on the minds of all those who have the welfare of their homes at heart. We claim three distinct features for **Persiatic Carpet Powder:** It disinfects rooms, purifies the air, destroys disease germs in carpets and clothing, and destroys moths and other insects that infest houses.

All goods manufactured by us have our trade mark, which is a guarantee of their purity and of the claims made for them. **Price, 25 cents.**

Persiatic Hot House
Fumigating
Powder

Awarded Bronze Medal and Diplomas, Toronto, Otta-wa, London, Sherbrooke.

The purpose in placing Persiatic Hot House Fumigating Powder before the public has been to fill a want that all Garden-ers, Hot House owners, and persons growing House plants have been as yet unable to fill. The burning of tobacco stems is a most disagreeable and tedious task. Persiatic Hot House Fumi-gating Powder is the pure extract of tobacco, prepared in such a manner as to make it far more effective than the burning of the ordinary tobacco stems, and which cannot possibly be done in any room in the house. But with Persiatic Hot House Fumi-gating Powder it is not only possible, but has the advantage of disinfecting the room or building in which used. One-half pound

Persiatic Fumigating Powder costs 25 cents, which is twice as cheap as tobacco stems, and is far more penetrating and effective and not as injurious to the plants as the burning tobacco stems. Persiatic Hot House Fumigating Powder is manufactured at our own Factories and Laboratories. All goods manufactured by us bear our own trade marks and designs, which is a guarantee of strength and purity.

Price—Half lb. tin, 25 cents ; One lb. tin, 50 cts.

PERSIATIC BED-BUG EXTERMINATOR

Bronze Medal and Diplomas at Toronto, London, Ottawa and Sherbrooke, Que

Is manufactured by a process only known to ourselves, and has been placed on the market for the purpose of exterminating bed-bugs —a horror to every self-respecting and up-to-date house-keeper. This bottle contains the pure crystals and oil of imported tobacco. The large demand for Persiatic Bed-Bug Exterminator is a guarantee of its effectiveness. **Price, 25 cents.**

Persiatic Pig Wash.

A prominent breeder has adopted the practice of dipping his pigs when from 4 to 12 weeks old, and claims that it is a great benefit. We give his experience in his own words :

Having a number of pigs, I noticed that when 8 to 10 weeks old, old enough to wean, some of them were not doing just as I would like to have them ; some of them were lousy, some a little mangy, and others looked measleyfied ; I had used kerosene and it did not have the desired effect. I was disappointed, but had some Persiatic Pig Wash in store, seeing it was good for lice and mange and skin diseases in Pigs, concluded to try it on the pigs in the following manner :

I put in a barrel 25 gallons of water and one quart of dip, and stirred it up good, then dipped the pigs. Never saw such a change ; not over 15 minutes' work. Left barrel in pen, and whenever I saw a pig the least wrong in the skin, I dumped it in the barrel of dip. I have the cleanest, nicest lot of shoats ever raised, and advise all raisers of hogs to try it. Dip your pigs several times at 4 to 12 weeks old and see for yourselves. It will more than save the price in feed, better growth ; kills all lice and humor in skin, besides disinfects them.

The subject of Dipping Pigs has come prominently before both breeders of fine or high-grade pigs and also breeders for market purposes. The above clipping is one of many experiences, and we may say as pioneers of introducing the Persiatic Pig Wash, made specially to meet the requirements of the pig, we have been successful beyond all expectations in the sale of Persiatic Pig Wash. Unsolicited testimonials speak for themselves, of which the following is a fair sample :

STOUFFVILLE, ONT., December 9th, 1898.
THE PICKHARDT RENFREW CO., Stouffville, Ont.

Gentlemen,—Some time ago I was induced to buy a can of your Persiatic Pig Wash, as I was advised it was a perfect insect destroyer of all kinds of vermin on live stock. I have a number of pigs, which were simply infested with lice. so much that when feeding they had to frequently stop and scratch themselves. I made one application of your Persiatic Pig Wash, as per directions, and I am very pleased to say that in three days time the change in the pigs was so noticeable that I made it my business to tell my neighbors about the splendid results. It simply cleaned the lice out, made the pigs rest and eat in comfort, and certainly acts like a tonic. I would advise washing pigs from time to time with Persiatic Pig Wash, lice or no lice. It does them good, they seem to relish the results.

J. A. TODD, Grain Merchant, Stouffville.

18

We have studied the peculiar action of different dips on pigs, and found that although the results of dips used were apparently satisfactory, we concluded that a dip specially prepared for pigs would be more satisfactory than any other dip made for sheep, cattle or horses. It would be remembered that the skin and flesh of a pig is entirely different from that of a sheep, cow or horse. One might as well say, take a liniment made for a horse and use it on man. Undoubtedly it would relieve the pain it was intended to remove and probably it would remove a good chunk of skin and flesh where applied on man. The comparison between a sheep skin and a pig skin is equal to a comparison between a horse skin and human skin. The action of a sheep, cattle or horse wash would be equal in results as above comparison, but in a different manner. The effect would not be noticeable directly, but its influence (the sheep wash used on a pig) would show itself, if use is persisted in, by producing cracked skin. This condition in a Pig is highly detrimental, causing slow growth, loss of appetite, and if pigs are ready for market, a loss of at least. 1c. per lb., and often making them unsaleable. A box sunk in ground, large enough to have a full sized pig covered with liquid when standing in box, water tight, with lid securely fastened when not in use will be found of great advantage and benefit. A monthly dipping of pigs, we believe, and experience shows it, will pay many times over for the slight expense and trouble gone to.

Persiatic Pig Wash is put up in 25c., 50c. and $1 cans, and is for sale at all stores.

TRI-JET, The Cyclone Sprayer . . .

THROWS THREE STREAMS

Patent
Applied
For.

MANUFACTURED BY THE

Pickhardt Renfrew Co., Limited, Stouffville, Ont., Canada

Use Persiatic Plant Spray. All Paris Green mixtures are dangerous and should be avoided.

It is Sure Death to Potato Bugs
In some sections Paris Green is first mixed with flour or land plaster and applied with a sifter. This is not only laborious and costly, but the operator is often made ill by breathing the dust charged with the poison. The advantage of our Sprayer over that method is obvious. The objection to the use of poisoned water when used in the ordinary sprayer or sprinkler has been the waste of material. It was impossible to thoroughly saturate the vine without wasting ten times

as much liquid as would remain to poison the bugs. By the use of our Sprayer a fine cloud-like spray reaches every portion of the vine and leaves it saturated, just as foliage appears after a fog. Bugs don't eat half a dozen leaves before they receive their "death blow." If you raise potatoes you can't afford to be without the Cyclone Sprayer.

WHY OUR SPRAYER IS BETTER THAN OTHERS OF SIMILAR CONSTRUCTION:

1st.—Because the reservoir is galvanized iron, and will not cor ode or rust.

2nd.—Because the feeding tubes are brass, and will not corrode or rust.

3rd.—Because the plunger is backed and reinforced by metal (not wood), which is shaped to the natural conformation of the leather washer when in action.

4th.—Because the end of the air chamber is metal and detachable.

5th.—Because it has three openings and three times the capacity of the ordinary single jet sprayer.

6th.—Because the sprayer is larger and will spray farther.

A careful comparison of the TRI-JET CYCLONE SPRAYER, point by point with other hand sprayers, is all that is needed to convince a man it is "THE BEST SPRAYER MADE."

FOR SHRUBS AND VINES

The Cyclone Sprayer is no less adapted to use in treating vines and shrubs of all kinds, such as Rose Bushes, Currant Bushes, Grape Vines, etc. The Cyclone Sprayer can also be used in blowing hellebore or other dry powder upon Rose Bushes Currant Bushes, etc., and is more effective than any other blower on the market. Use Persiatic Plant Spray.

If you cultivate flowers or small fruits, you can't afford to be without the Cyclone Sprayer.

IT IS USED IN THE HENNERY.—There is no sprayer which will accomplish half so much in cleaning the "hen-house" of lice and other vermin. You can't make hens lay and breed lice at the same time. If you raise hens you can't afford to be without the Cyclone Sprayer. Use Persiatic Hen House Spray.

FOR FLIES ON CATTLE AND HORSES —It is a well-known fact that cows cannot give a good flow of milk in the summer time when they are pestered with flies. From an economical standpoint, as well as humane, it is to the interest of every farmer to spray his cattle with cattle oil or some of the many preparations for keeping off flies. The Cyclone Sprayer will do it cheaper and better than any other. Use Persiatic Cattle Fly Spray.

BELLECHASSE COUNTY, QUE., JUNE 1, 1898.

DEAR SIRS,—I have been using a common sprayer during the last two years, spraying potato bugs,and I find it is the best instrument or machine for that purpose. Although mine is worth more than any-thing known before, I must say that the Sprayer Mr. Lacroix is show-ing me is far better and more complete than mine. I recommend it to the public as the best machine of that kind, and by so doing I am confident I will be doing the farmers a great favor. Yours truly,
JOSEPH CASGRAIN.

Mr. Desire Lamontague, of Bellechasse County, Que., says :

For the two weeks I have been using the Sprayer I got from you I don't hesitate to tell you that it has paid for itself several times by the economy I have realized on Paris Green. I can tell you that this small apparatus is one of the best of all agricultural ma-chines. and I don't know how anyone who tried it could say other-wise, for it is light and very easy to handle, so that a child can do the work as well as a man. I use from 10 to 15 pounds of Paris Green each year, but this season 1 ½ or 2 pounds was enough. Useless to say I am very well satisfied with it.

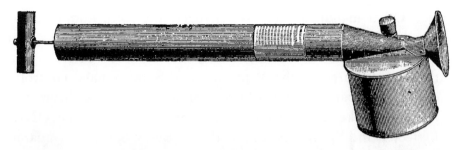

The Mitchell Hand Sprayer.

The best and cheapest Sprayer on the market. Throws the finest spray of any sprayer made. This machine, which is very strong and highly polished, is made of the best quality of material that can be procured, and only the best workmen are employed.

A Few Questions Answered Concerning Hand Sprayers

No. 1.—What is a Perfect Hand Sprayer? Answer.—A Sprayer which throws a perfect spray of either liquid or dry powder.

No. 2.—Who was the original inventor of the Hand Sprayer? Answer.—C. H. Mitchell, of Utica, N.Y., first invented and perfected the Hand Sprayer in Utica, N.Y., in February, 1896, and since that time this Sprayer has been introduced to the largest florists, gardeners and fruit growers throughout the United States and Canada who have tested it and given it the highest recommendation. It throws a spray as fine as a cloud of smoke, which being damp adheres to the plant, completely covering every portion with the poison. It is light, easy to handle, and does more rapid work than any other sprayer. It will be necessary for every household in the land to have one of these machines when its value is known. The capacity of work for which it is adapted is unlimited. We only ask that a trial be made to show its value. There is no insect living that it will not destroy when the proper liquids are used. We also furnish recipes with each sprayer, which will kill all hugs and insects injurious to plant life.

Other manufacturers have changed the form and manufactured so-called Sprayers under other names. They look all right, but why is it they do not give satisfaction? The reason is that the manufacturers of the Mitchell Hand Sprayer have control of certain vital parts without which a Sprayer will not throw that fine smoke-like spray which stamps the Mitchell as the ONLY Perfect Hand Sprayer on the market. Every Sprayer is guaranteed to do perfect work. Even competitors pay tribute to the excellency of our Sprayer by copying our 1897 circulars in their 1899 catalogues.

What the Secretary of the Ontario Fruit Experimental Station says :

GRIMSBY, November 8, 1898.

GENTLEMEN,—I have been using the Mitchell Hand Sprayer at this station during the past season for destroying thrips, aphidis, fungi, potato beetles, and all such enemies of the gardener, and find it the most convenient thing in the garden I ever handled. The large orchard pumps are too cumbersome for the garden, and this one is so light and convenient and always ready for use. I have several orchard pumps, but would not be without this Hand Sprayer for four times its cost.   L. WOOLVERTON, M.A.

AS A POTATO-BUG KILLER THIS MACHINE HAS NO EQUAL. ONE GALLON OF THE PERSIATIC PLANT SPRAY MIXTURE IS SUFFICIENT FOR AN ACRE OF POTATOES. AVOID PARIS GREEN.

THE PICKHARDT RENFREW CO, LIMITED,
STOUFFVILLE, ONT., CANADA, General Agents.

THE SPRAMOTOR

PAINTING, WHITEWASHING & SPRAYING MACHINE

HEARD'S PATENTS: CANADA, 1895, 1897 ; U.S., 1899.

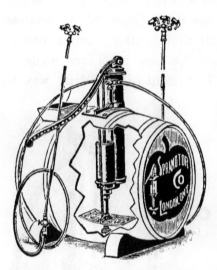

" The law is that the agricultural schools and farms shall aid the farmer by means of experiments, farm managements, investigations of special difficulties, by lectures, publications and teaching. This has been done, yet we found it to be a fact that the majority of the farmers have not been personally touched by these great enterprises. Much of the teaching is necessarily too advanced to appeal to the general farmer. Scientific knowledge is far in advance of the best farm practice. The farmer must be awakened and educated. How ?"

The above extract from Bulletin 159, January, 1899, published by the Cornell University Experimental Station, aptly expresses the difficulty attending any effort to reach the farmers.

In Canada we believe the farmers are in advance of their fellows in any country in the world, and are to a greater extent than others putting the knowledge obtained from scientific experiment to practical use. The farmers of Ontario have certainly been awakened to the advantages of spraying, which is mainly owing to the efforts of the Department of Agriculture, during the past five years, in demonstrating to them, in various places throughout the province, the proper way to spray. The Department at the outset came to the conclusion that if success was to be attained they must have good machines to work with, and in order to settle the much disputed point as to which was the best spraying apparatus, invited all the manufacturers of spraying appliances to come and test their machines in actual work, under judges appointed by the Fruit Growers' Association of Ontario, which was done by all those having confidence in their apparatus, and which included the best machines made in Canada and the United States. The result of this trial was to

effectually dispel all doubt as to which appliance was the best, and proved that there was no longer need of going out of Canada for spraying appliances, but rather that the Americans were so completely excelled that they are now importing spraying apparatus from the Spramotor Co., even against an almost prohibitive duty.

This trial, placing as it did the Spramotor first, has saved the farmers and fruit growers of Canada thousands of dollars by preventing them from buying poor, cheap and hard-working pumps, which have done more to discourage the practice of spraying than all other causes combined, as well as the consequent loss and disgust in their use.

Our object in this catalogue is to show the various spraying apparatus that are made and patented by us and sold under the name "Spramotor," which is a new coined word owned by us for trade mark purposes. All goods sold under this name are fully warranted first-class from a standpoint of workmanship and materials, and guaranteed to give complete satisfaction in competent hands, for we will cheerfully take back any goods sent out by us that prove faulty in any respect, returning the money paid for them or replacing them with perfect machines.

JUDGES' OFFICIAL AWARD.

This is to certify that at the contest of Spraying Apparatus, held at Grimsby under the auspices of the Board of Control of the Fruit Experimental Stations of Ontario, in which there were eleven contestants, the Spramotor, made by the Spramotor Co., of London, Ont., was awarded FIRST PLACE.

H. L. HUTT,
M. PETTIT,
Judges.

Since the contest, the details of the Spramotor has been greatly changed and improved. A new compensating plunger, new nozzles, new attachments for strainer, new hand valve, drip guard, and an entirely new machine in three sizes — the Spramotor Jr.—has been invented and added. We have also patented an attachment for making mechanical kerosene mixtures, completely doing away with the old style kerosene emulsion.

The Spramotor has grown and appropriated the attention of those best qualified to know what a spraying equipment should be, not only in Canada, but in the United States as well, and is due to the fact that, before commencing to manufacture, exhaustive scientific experiments were made by the inventor, who is an expert mechanical engineer as well as an extensive fruit grower, wherein all the various features that go to make up a spraying equipment, were thoroughly tested in actual work, with the result that what was thought impossible by the old-line makers of spraying apparatus is daily demonstrated in the Spramotor.

DEPARTMENT OF AGRICULTURE, ONTARIO,
TORONTO, AUG. 28, 1896.

DEAR SIR,—I have great pleasure in stating that the Spramotor ordered from your Company this season has given entire satisfaction. It works easily, and is very effective in its operation. Your Company deserves much credit for placing so excellent a pump on the market.

Yours very truly,
JNO. DRYDEN,
Minister of Agriculture.

Mr. W. H. Heard, Manager of Spramotor Co., London, Ont.

In constructing the Spramotor the inventor recognized the fact that no apparatus existed which could use the various spraying mixtures without serious and rapid deterioration. The effort made to supply the need and combine the expert knowledge of the mechanic with the practical experience of the orchardist is seen in the universal approval with which the Spramotor has been received, being pronounced by all the various authorities as being the first successful effort to supply a practical working machine that completely fills the requirements.

The cost of spraying having been reduced to such a low figure, it need not cost the fruit grower any anxiety, as the results are so clearly in favor of the operation. In fact, intelligent people no longer question the advisability of spraying. They have learned that their fruit and crops can be saved by spraying, at an expense that is relatively trifling. No successful orchardist or progressive farmer needs to-day to be told that in order to obtain sound fruit, or indeed in many cases any fruit at all, he must adopt the best available means of destroying both fungi and insect pests. When spraying trees and shrubs always use Persiatic Tree Spray: Avoid Paris Green—it is dangerous and in time will kill your trees.

Note what the largest manufacturer of farm implements under the British flag says :

TORONTO, 9th Nov., 1898.

SPRAMOTOR COMPANY, London, Ont.

Gentlemen,—The machines for spraying and whitewashing you have supplied to Dentonia Park Farm have done their work well, and are quite satisfactory. I could not have believed there was so much value in spraying fruit trees. We had a good crop of apples, where-as our neighbors, who used no spraying apparatus, had practically none. Yours truly,

W. E. H. MASSEY.

The Willowmead Fumigator

A Practical Apparatus for Vaporizing Fluid or Solid Insecticides, Disinfectants and Medicinal Agents.

(Patent Applied for.)

Powerful, Safe, Durable, Convenient, Simple, Effective and Inexpensive.

Needed by every Flower Grower, Physician, Board of Health and Private Sanitarium.

* It displaces kerosene stoves, red-hot irons and other inconvenient, ineffective and dangerous appliances. In its improved, simplified form this veritable "Little Giant" will be found to fill a widespread need as a means of generating fumes or vapors destructive to germs or mature forms of Greenhouse Pests, and Fungoid and other parasites producing injury or disease in plants

or man. Its evolution has been the result of much study and experiment to furnish an effective, yet inexpensive and convenient means for producing the desired result. It consists of only three parts, viz. : A combined base, lamp, cup and handle ; a lamp burner ; and a combined concentrating cylinder and evaporating pan. Wood alcohol is used to generate heat in it, one cent's worth of which will evaporate two fluid ounces of the preparation used. The peculiar form of this apparatus allows of a quick and convenient filling of the lamp cup, concentrates and centers the the flame on the bottom of the evaporating pan, and prevents waste of heat from side drafts. Such air as is needed for combustion, and no more, is drawn up and around the lamp cup, keeping it cool. A ridge around the base catches any accidental overflow of the fluids used. The peculiar manner of connecting the handle with the base of the apparatus keeps it cool for handling. The tall cylinder concentrates and conserves the heat and allows of its being handled by its lower and cool part. Ordinary candle wick or a rolled kerosene lamp wick is used in the burner. All the parts are very durable, being made of cast iron, galvanized iron and copper. It will last a lifetime. A number can be carried by their handles in each hand and quickly distributed and operated in any greenhouse, dwelling or apartment.

This apparatus is not a toy. It is constructed for practical work. Being inexpensive, a number can be conveniently operated and thus an effective and abundant supply of the vapor or gas used can be quickly generated wherever needed ; be that in closets, corners or open spaces.

Physicians will find this apparatus invaluable for disinfecting their clothing in a closet or small room after visiting contagious cases. It will economically and quickly evaporize formaldehyde or any other disinfectant. This fumigator will be found the most effective apparatus for disinfecting dwellings schools, hospitals, cars, vessels, hotels, etc. They can be used to destroy insects and germs in bedrooms, kitchens, laundry, hen-houses and stables. *As a bedside generator of pure or medicated aqueous vapor it is invaluable.* To the plant-man and flower grower the Willowmead Fumigator will be found indispensable to disseminate any of the concentrated fungicides or insecticides in vapor or gaseous form, either in the greenhouse, disinfecting closet or plant tent. By using several fumigators two or more insecticidal agents can be generated and applied at one time, and the vapors or gases may be evenly diffused, and thus effects secured not otherwise attainable.

Price, $2.25; per case of six fumigators, $12.00. Orders must be accompanied by cash in the form of postal or express orders drawn in favor of the manufacturers.

Special attention is called to the Persiatic Fumigating Powders and Persiatic Fumigating Liquids put up by the Pickhardt Renfrew, Co. of Stouffville, Ont, Canada, especially adapted for use in Hot Houses, Outbuildings, Hospitals, and Homes.